Then & Now
WHITEHAVEN

Whitehaven town centre seen from above the Crossthwaite Memorial School, 1998.

Then & Now
WHITEHAVEN

Compiled by Alan W. Routledge

One of the many parades to swing round the Duke Street/Tangier Street corner over the past 350 years. This one took place in 1941, during war weapons week, to promote the donation of money to help buy guns and munitions to use against the Nazis in those dark and early days of the war. The people of Whitehaven raised £35,000 and purchased a Spitfire named *Scawfell* which fought in the battle of Britain. Who remembers the Rubber Shop (now part of Whittles) or where the air-raid shelter was located?

First published in 1999 by Tempus Publishing
Reprinted 2003

Reprinted in 2009 by
The History Press
The Mill, Brimscombe Port,
Stroud, Gloucestershire, GL5 2QG
www.thehistorypress.co.uk

British Library Cataloguing in Publication Data.
A catalogue record for this book is available from the British Library.

ISBN 978 0 7524 1601 4

Typesetting and origination by Tempus Publishing
Printed and bound in England

Contents

The Queen's Cinema was one of three in the town, the others being the Empire and the Gaiety. Of these only the latter now remains in use. The open space to the left of the cinema was redeveloped into a much disliked multi-storey car park; built at a cost of £670,000, it opened in late spring of 1973. The Queen's was demolished at the same time and the site became a Presto superstore, later renamed Safeway. This, in turn, has relocated to the Flatt Walks and the building now stands empty.

Acknowledgements

The author wishes to record his sincere thanks to the following, whose input has been of great help in the compilation of this book:

Albright & Wilson Ltd, and in particular Mr Alan Taylor, Human Resources Manager at the Marchon Works here in Whitehaven; The Beacon on West Strand for allowing me access to their large photographic archives; British Nuclear Fuels PLC, for the wonderful aerial photographs of the Sellafield Site; Jimmy O'Neil of Bransty, whose collection of old photographs and postcards proved to be especially useful; Ray Devlin, for all his help and encouragement, particularly with regard to mining.

Lastly, but by no means the least, my thanks to Frances, my wife, who has had much to put with over the past few months.

Introduction

When first approached to compile a book of ninety or so old photographs of Whitehaven and compare them with a similar number of new pictures, the task seemed to be fairly straightforward. With access to several thousand negatives in The Beacon's photographic archive together with a similar number of my own, nothing could be simpler – such naivety is now hard to credit.

Whitehaven has so far had a relatively short life-span, barely 500 years, but it has been a time packed with history and change. Regrettably a great deal of this historical metamorphosis has not been recorded on photographic plate or film. Nevertheless a sufficient number of pictures were taken and have survived to the present day; permitting the publication of more than a dozen books of photographs of old Whitehaven over the past few years.

The purpose of *Whitehaven Then & Now* is to illustrate the changes which have occurred within the community over a period of years; changes to both bricks and mortar and to the social and economic welfare of its people. During the image selection process it was necessary to search for pictures which not only illustrated the changes which have taken place but also had not been previously published. It was this latter condition that made the task difficult. The generosity of other collectors has been overwhelming! Thanks to them, the majority of images in *Whitehaven Then & Now* have not appeared in any other publication.

Production of the modern versions of each image should have been a simple affair. All that was needed was to load the camera with film, set off with a list of requirements, point the lens, press the button and the picture's in the bag. Making use of modern photographic equipment ought also to have facilitated my task. However, standing in the middle of Lowther, King or Duke Streets turned out to be a perilous business and the setting up of a tripod in the centre of the road was not an option. Traffic was the problem with shoppers searching endlessly for a place to park and taxi drivers constantly looking for a fare! Surely the phenomena of modern day vehicular traffic must be the greatest manifestation of change anywhere one cares to look throughout the British Isles.

In 1900 there were close to 400 shops in Whitehaven, today there is barely a third of that number. Most have given way to that other newcomer – the supermarket. Many of the town's former emporiums have become the offices of building societies, insurance societies, estate agents, and an ever growing number of fast food outlets and takeaways together with their attendant wheely bins and hungry pigeons and seagulls. Fortunately many of Whitehaven's fine Georgian buildings remain, although, in some cases, there has been a degree of renovation. The town centre streets were carefully laid out in a grid system dating back to the days of Sir Christopher, Sir John and Sir James Lowther. Changes to the original grid have occurred but these have been kept to a minimum. Pedestrianization of some streets (to make life a little easier for the shopper) and some street widening (to ease traffic congestion) have been the greatest changes. While many of the buildings, fronting onto the main streets, have remained untouched the poorer quality, in-fill properties behind have all been cleared away, and their occupants moved to estates on the outskirts of town.

During the seventeenth, eighteenth and nineteenth centuries, the harbour was only developed when it was of direct benefit to Lowther family interests. The two magnificent piers were completed in the 1840s and the wet dock was commissioned some thirty years later. This was too little and too late for the town's merchants and traders who left the area preferring towns with deep water harbours and easy access to large

Over the centuries Whitehaven provided soldiers for the local militia and later for the county regiment – 'The 34th of foot' latterly called The Border Regiment. In 1972 it was merged with the Lancaster-based King's Own Royal Regiment to form a new modern battalion which has recently seen service in many of the world's trouble spots including Belize, Bosnia, Northern Ireland and Kosovo. This photograph was taken during the Borders final parade through Whitehaven, with the soldiers wearing uniforms from times past.

centres of population. Whitehaven's loss was Liverpool and Glasgow's gain! It was not until the Marchon Chemical Works started to import phosphate rock from Morocco that further development of the harbour side occurred and for the best part of thirty years giant silos and a large conveyor system dominated the skyline. Lorries rolled endlessly through the streets and, needless to say, this was not to everybody's liking. In 1993 the last load of rock was imported and the silos and conveyor system removed, in their place a new building has been erected for HM Inland Revenue. A new sea-lock and marina have been completed – these are the foundations upon which the 'Renaissance of Whitehaven' project firmly rests.

Industrially, Whitehaven has changed with equal speed. Gone are the coal mines, shipbuilding, iron manufacture, salt production, anhydrite and alabaster mining, quarrying, glass and pottery making, together with many inter-dependant industries. These have been replaced, as major sources of a living wage, by the likes of Albright & Wilson Ltd, British Nuclear Fuels Limited and the High-Tec units at West Lakes, together with a host of smaller, service suppliers. Naturally these changes have had a significant effect on the social well being of the town's population. Changes here have occurred within the spheres of education, health care and leisure.

To some extent it has been possible to depict these changes visually and several informative images, which have survived the passage of time, form the basis of this book. They also serve to remind us that over the years, ordinary family photographs will become important records of our local history and should be carefully stored for future reference together with as much information about them as is possible.

Alan W. Routledge, 1999

Chapter 1

The Harbour

Whitehaven Harbour, *c.* 1950. Seen from the Mount, the harbour was still a busy place in the years immediately following the Second World War. There are several vessels in the Queen's Dock with yet another rounding the 'Devil's Elbow'. All are in the harbour to load coal for Dublin or Belfast. On that bright summer day William Pit was still in production and the town gas-holders were full. Today these are no longer a feature of the urban landscape, nor is The Beacon Flour Mills. The shed piled high with fish boxes is also a thing of the past.

Although fishing has been part of the harbour's day to day activity for many years, this was not always the case. The fishing fleet was based at Barrowmouth between 1675 and 1750, and in 1685 Sir John Lowther gave the fishing fleet £25 to built a sheltered landing there. Later called Port Hamilton, it was to accommodate fifteen fishing cobles and allow landing in all but the roughest of weather. The old photograph dates from 1890 and shows the Whitehaven registered fishing boats – WA13 and WA55. The Lime Tongue was used for the loading of domestic ashes and 'night-soil' for disposal at sea via a special barge, *The Redness Point*. The dumping of domestic and industrial waste at sea was still taking place as late as the 1950s. The newer image shows a visiting fishing trawler getting under way.

The Merchant's Quay was used as the station for the Isle of Man and Liverpool Steam Passenger Boat services and a couple of these boats are shown at the Merchant's Quay, *c.* 1900. Until last year the quay was used by many fishing boats often tied up in line abreast and it was possible to walk across the Custom's House Dock without getting one's feet wet. Today the quay has lost the shed which at one time ran down its full length, keeping both passengers and their luggage dry. At the moment the quay is covered with ice-making plant, fuel tanks and other paraphernalia of the fishing industry however, it is planned to clear the quay of all these buildings and materials as part of harbour improvements.

Fishermen caught the fish, and their families cleaned and filleted them, either for direct sale to the public or for preserving in salt or pickle. In 1905 one such family is pictured setting up on the West Strand. The Strand was well known for the number of pubs it contained. The Royal Standard, The Ship, The Rose and Thistle, The Manx Smack and The Steam Packet House were all well patronized until the 1930s. The Electricity Generating Station, seen in the background of the older image, has been carefully restored and is now used as a pumping station by North West Water. The area on which the fish sellers stood is soon to be converted into a public arena for open-air theatre, art and other displays. 'The Hub' will have a removable, weather-proof cover which will add to its versatility.

Coal was exported through the port of Whitehaven for more than 300 years and initially this was handled at the hurries and staithes located on the West Strand. In later years a new handling facility was constructed on the Queen's Dock and exports to Ireland continued until the 1980s. The older image, around 1935, shows a typical coaster of that period loading out in the Queen's Dock. Loading was simply a matter of dropping coal from a rail wagon down a chute into the boat, which would move its position from time to time to allow even distribution of the load. Today the chute and rail sidings have been removed and the quay is used by The Range Boat and a three-masted sailing boat awaiting renovation.

This fine old painting of a steam paddle tug, (possibly the *Refuge*) towing three collier vessels out into the outer harbour, illustrates just how busy the port used to be. Fully laden vessels could only leave Whitehaven when wind and tide were right, so a tow out of the harbour speeded matters up and cleared the hurries for further business. The tug is passing the watchtower and harbourmaster's office. The Old Quay and The Devil's Elbow have recently been joined to form a large sea lock which allows access to the harbour for four hours either side of high tide. Thanks to the lock the whole of the inner harbour is now permanently under water.

This steam paddle tug was custom built for Whitehaven Harbour in 1862 by C. & W. Earle of Hull and on arrival was registered as the *Prince of Wales*. It is shown tied up outside the Queen's Dock around 1875. After re-boilering in 1880 by Fletcher Jennings of Lowca the tug continued in service for some years before disappearing from the record books. A point of interest is the number of rail wagons loaded with timber newly arrived from Scandinavia. Today the harbour has no tug boat and when one is needed it has to be specially hired for the job. One such tug, the *Frances*, was seen in Whitehaven recently.

Whitehaven is a tidal harbour prone to silting, particularly when big tides and strong winds combine to stir up the muddy bottom. In the early years the problem was tackled by men with picks and shovels and teams of horses and carts. Eventually the Harbour Commissioners introduced a bucket elevator type of floating dredger which remained in service until *The Clearway* was purchased in 1928. When she retired in 1993 she was the oldest steam-powered dredger still in working order. *The Clearway* has since gone for scrap. Recent dredging of the harbour, necessary for the new lock and leisure developments, has been carried out by *The Wyre*, which was hired for the purpose and is pictured in action.

Fishing has to some extent dominated activities in the old Customs House Dock but even in the early 1900s there was some sailing for pleasure and checking the boat out prior to sailing often attracted the attention of the curious youngster. In the background, alongside the Lime Tongue, the barge *Redness Point* is piled high with the contents of the town's dustbins and ash pits ready for towing out and dumping at sea. Today the Customs House Dock has had its floor levelled and is soon to be part of the marina complex. The Lime Tongue, on the other hand, will have a wave, sculptured in metal, running along its length.

making their own detergent materials. On 3 October 1963 Alan Birkett (chemical engineer) and Alan W. Routledge (commissioning engineer) arrived in Volgodonsk to carry out pre-commissioning checks. They were later joined by: Martin Rowe, Ron Fogg (project managers), John Bainbridge, Jimmy Mitchell, Eddie Thompson, Jeff Waite (chemical engineers), Cyril Gordon, Jimmy Martin (shift engineers), Ernie Sanderson, Billy Telford (shift managers), Reg Fell and Tommy Thornton (analytical chemists). Today this part of the harbour stands silent except for a new pleasure boat lift which, once the new marina is in full use, should assure the harbour's future for some considerable time to come.

Marchon Products Limited are not just importers, they also export a significant quantity of the materials they produce; indeed their efforts have been so successful that the company has been awarded The Queen's Award for Export Achievement on a number of occasions. In the 1950s and '60s goods were exported to Eastern Europe directly from Whitehaven and a Polish vessel loading up with packets of detergent for Gdansk can be seen here. Currency problems made trade with Eastern Europe difficult and this led Marchon to sell Russia the technical know-how for

During 1954 Marchon Products Limited began to import phosphate rock from Casablanca, Morocco for use in the phosphoric acid manufacturing plant at their Ladysmith Works. At first the rock was brought in by chartered vessels but such was the demand for phosphates that the company soon had three ships of its own involved in the trade – *The Marchon Trader*, *The Venturer* and *The Enterprise*. The rock was unloaded directly from the boats into an endless stream of lorries, such this one operated by Millers of Whitehaven. Importation of phosphate rock ceased in 1993 and today the quayside stands idle. It is part of the harbour which has been set aside for a Yacht Club or similar venture, aimed at catering for the visiting leisure time sailor.The installation of the first batch of floating pontoons has been completed and the level of interest in the new facilities is such that the available berths are already three parts occupied. The harbour has, in effect, gone full circle; sail, steam power, mechanical power and back to sail again! However this time the crews of these modern wind-powered vessels sail for pleasure and not for the profits to be made from some exotic cargo.

From the earliest days the harbour was used for the transportation of passengers; soldiers and cavalry to Ireland and, during the Jacobean uprisings, Irish Protestant refugees to Whitehaven on the return leg. Later there were regular passenger services to the Isle of Man, Belfast, Carlisle, Dublin, Liverpool and Scotland. Such was the popularity of these steam packets that sailings were a daily occurrence. The ships, with names like *Mona's Isle*, *Magdelena*, *Saint Andrew* and *The Countess of Lonsdale*, could not help but add to the romance of the voyage. The older photograph shows one Liverpool bound vessel leaving the Steam Boat Station on the Sugar Tongue. Today's passenger services have declined to just a couple of sailings, on bank holidays, from the North Pier aboard the restored paddle steamer, *Waverley,* or the ferry, *Balmoral*.

The use of silos for buffer storage and much larger cranes was not sufficient to meet the growing demand for more phosphate rock and a new method of importation was needed. Delivery by bulk carrier in loads of up to 30,000 tons, unloaded at sea and ferried in by the company's own vessels, provided the answer. A special barge the *Odin* was built in Moss, Norway to do the job and on its delivery two of the Marchon boats were sold. Just a few years ago the use of phosphate rock by the factory ceased and the silos and cranes fell into disuse. Today the silos and the conveyor system have gone and all that remains are the two decaying cranes.

The silos were considered an eyesore and the lorries rumbling though the town, night and day, were noisy and dirty! Nevertheless both elements played an important part in the economic health of Marchon and the town's traders also profited through the workers' wage packets. This part of the harbour has long been associated with local industry. It was where the following men started the shipbuilding industry: Thomas Sibson (1686-1775), Joseph White (1714-1766), Rodger Martindale (died 1784) and William Palmer (1702-1778). This continued until work on the Queen's Dock commenced in 1872. Once the dock was opened in 1876 coal shipments were transferred and the hurries were closed for good. Later Marchon built its silos there. To the left of the silos are the Queen's Dock loading chutes together with a train load of coal waiting for shipment to Ireland. The final load of coal to be moved by ship from Whitehaven left the harbour in the early 1980s and the last phosphate rock was off-loaded in 1993. The site was levelled in 1997 and Blencathra House was erected, designed and built to look like a Georgian warehouse, the office block is the preserve of the Inland Revenue.

Chapter 2

Streets and Buildings

Whitehaven was built to a series of strict guidelines; the streets to be laid out in the form of a grid, the buildings to be properly aligned and to have the same number of storeys. Lowther Street was the widest and had the grandest buildings, located in such a way that the view from the castle to the harbour was unimpaired. This is the view looking down Lowther Street towards the harbour in 1933. It is interesting to note that much of the Old Quay and the Devil's Elbow are painted white. Road traffic is notable by its virtual absence.

Of all Whitehaven's buildings the castle is probably the most significant. It was built by Sir George Fletcher of Hutton and sold to Sir John Lowther in 1675. The Flatt, as it was then known, was substantially altered to meet Lowther's own needs and during 1769 Sir James Lowther completely rebuilt it and called it Whitehaven Castle. The castle was purchased by Hurbert W. Walker in 1923 and donated, together with a considerable sum of money, to the people of Whitehaven for use as a hospital. The Infirmary was absorbed into the newly created National Health Service in 1948 and remained in use until a purpose built hospital was erected at Hensingham in 1956. Unfortunately the castle had been allowed to fall into disrepair, causing a great deal of disquiet to the local populace. However, a contract has recently been signed and money granted which will allow the castle to be restored and converted to flats and offices.

Perhaps the least altered area in Whitehaven is Lowther Street. It was here that many of the town's most wealthy merchants built their mansions and houses. The near left-hand side of the street has seen the greatest degree of rebuilding. Gone are The Granary, The Museum and The White Bull Inn; replacing them are The County Library and Civic Halls. Nearer to the camera is the new Safeway superstore, together with its car parks and petrol station. Most of the other properties have seen changes in the nature of their business activities while the volume of traffic coming into town, down Lowther Street, has necessitated both traffic lights and filter lanes at its junctions with Scotch Street.

The Whitehaven Co-operative Society Ltd started at No. 21 Duke Street in 1875 and remained on the site until it merged with the Cleator Moor Co-op, from which time the business continued in new, larger premises at the corner of Duke and Tangier Streets. The shop was later occupied by J.A. Woodnorth (grocer) and Robert Woodnorth (painter and decorator). The grocery business was purchased in 1925 by Thomas E. Bell who moved from No. 21 Church Street where he was a partner in Ferguson and Bell (grocers). Tom Bell and Bob Woodnorth traded from Duke Street until they were forced to leave during the town centre clearance scheme of 1956. Mr Bell and his assistant are pictured standing in front of one of the shops in the 1930s. The clearance and road widening work led to the demolition of part of No. 21 and the whole of one side of Church Street. Later occupiers of No. 21 included Len Fletcher (jeweller and watchmaker) and The Past Times Tea Rooms.

We can be certain about when this photograph was taken – 11 July 1894 – the day of Whitehaven's Incorporation into a Borough. The large banner draped over Mr Davis' Chusan Tea & Coffee House states 'Success To Whitehaven and the Mayor'. The new status of a Borough brought the Lowther family's domination of Whitehaven to an end. This was a time of great rejoicing for the people of Whitehaven. The Chusan Tea House has been substantially altered at ground floor level and is now occupied by John Whittle (house furnishers) who are part of the Carlisle based Carl Vasey Group. Today this busy corner is protected by a couple of pelican crossings without which life, for the pedestrian, would be a great deal more difficult.

Opposite the Chusan Tea Rooms the Co-operative Society's grocery department opened in 1888. Shopping was more leisurely in those days with customer requirements noted in the dividend book and dealt with by both counter and accounts staff; the goods were often delivered to the door by errand boys. The fine old building has just been converted into a youth club, while the ground floor is the domain of the Chatanooga Pizza House offering fast food – also delivered to your door.

Duke Street has seen a great deal of change along its whole length, large areas having been demolished to make way for council flats and road widening. At the time the photograph was taken (around 1904) Strand Street was little more than a narrow lane. At present The Globe Hotel houses The Milano Pizza House and a café, while The Ship has become The John Paul Jones Inn and The Wheatsheaf is buried under the greatly widened Strand Street. Whitehaven Public Swimming Baths have relocated to Hensingham and the building has been converted into the Park Nite-Spot. The dock offices and clock have long been demolished and Louis Leefsen's hairdressing salon is now the local branch of the Citizen's Advice Bureau.

High King Street has seen many changes but when viewed from the Lowther Street junction, the most obvious difference is in the fashions of the day. Walter Holloway's toy shop and William Strathern's plumbers and glaziers have gone along with the Black Lion Hotel, whose licence to sell alcohol lapsed in 1932. Replacing them are Montegue Burton and Bon Marche. The latter premises were previously occupied by The New Century Stores and more recently by John Wade, house furnishers. The Black Lion was one of Whitehaven's oldest and more important hotels, catering for the weary traveller and local businessman alike. The early proprietors of the Burton's building applied for a billiards licence for the upstairs rooms. This upper floor also served as the local Income Tax Office until it moved to the newly built Mark House in the late 1950s.

King Street was once known as the 'Golden Mile' and it was said that anything from a pin to an elephant could be bought on the street, provided one had sufficient money! Several shops have gone to make way for F.W. Woolworth and the Halifax Building Society. Shops once to be found included (from right to left): No. 41 W.B. Dalzell (butcher), No. 40 The Maypole Dairy, No. 39 J.T. Colclough (hatter), No. 38 C.B. Dalzell (tobacconist), No. 37 F.B. Bennett (chemist), and No. 36 Fisher and Steward (wine and spirits merchants). The low fronted building further up the street was the Low Market, where shambles meat was sold. The Green Market has also changed; the properties occupied by Klick and Lite Bites were, in 1904, in the hands of Dixon & Co. (wholesale and retail fishmongers) and John Bull (butchers and ships suppliers).

The ancient Butter Market was demolished in 1883 and the present Market Hall built in its place. In the space of 100 years the building has found use as a covered market (for dairy produce), a cinema, a pram factory, an electrical goods wholesale warehouse, a museum, and at present houses the Tourist Information Centre together with a café, and the offices of the Whitehaven Development Company. For many years the building housed a public convenience so when it finally closed, in the 1960s, shoppers were put to some considerable inconvenience. The older photograph, from 1990, shows the building in its guise as a museum which, after a spell housed in the Civic Hall, is now located at The Beacon on the West Strand.

Nowhere in Whitehaven has changed as much as the Old Town area. Dating from the winter of 1972/73 the older photograph allows us a glimpse of the rear of the Market Place. Ladbrokes the bookmakers now occupies the Pinapple Hotel and tucked away in the background are the new flats on Charles, George, Michael, Peter and Queen Streets. On Scotch Street, the Congregational church has now been redeveloped into the police station and Magistrates Court but this modern building falls far short of the Georgian image the town is keen to preserve! The foreground once contained the Onion Warehouse, The Buck's Head Inn, Tommy Cowan's (firelighter works), The King's Arms, Herdman's (tinplaters) and Marchon Products' original factory. Today this old site is occupied by a rather plain multi-storey car park.

Whitehaven's original market charter was reconfirmed in 1660 and until recent times a market was held every Tuesday, Thursday and Saturday. The older photograph dates from the 1930s and although there are fewer stall-holders today, the market still attracts the careful bargain hunter. Safely underground these days, the Poe Beck flows down the length of the market. A new public toilet block, built in the neo-Georgian style, has replaced The Guinea Warehouse which, as it name suggests, was once connected to the slave trade. Open only during normal business hours, the new facility is far removed from the main stream of activity. Towards the left of the older picture is the old Refuge School. Originally funded by charitable donation, the school was replaced by the much bigger Crossthwaite Memorial School in 1901.

The Onion Warehouse in Swing Pump Lane was demolished soon after it was pictured, in the 1920s, to allow for the construction of the Queens Cinema. The cinema is no more, it was replaced by a supermarket which now stands empty. The building to the left of the warehouse was used as a grocery shop by Thomas Bowman and Sons and later by a house furnisher and upholsterer – John Leach. The Queens staged many of the Hospital Pantomime Society's productions and its Saturday afternoon matinees screened serials such as *Buck Rodgers*, *The Lone Ranger* and *The Mark of Zorro*. The site is now occupied in part by the superstore and in part by a multi-storey car park.

Seen here with members of his workforce in 1910, outside his Roper Street shop, is John Roan, a manufacturer, wholesaler and retailer of leather goods. The shop was dominated by a full-size, stuffed horse on which all kinds of saddlery was displayed. Ernest Burnyeat ran the shop as a saddlers and sports goods supplier from the 1920s until the building was demolished in 1974 at which time the business moved to Lowther Street. The Co-op superstore mopped up most of the block bounded by Queen, Roper, Church and Lowther Streets; only the latter remained untouched by the bulldozer. The Co-op superstore was built at a time when Whitehaven was waking up to the value of its heritage and the new building was expected to keep a Georgian exterior. However something seems to have been lost in the execution of that particular plan!

St Nicholas School, the fire station and the Congregational church were demolished to make way for a new police station and Magistrates Court, built in a modern style, from concrete, and far removed from the Georgian character of the street! The original police station and Magistrates Court buildings have been carefully restored and now house the County Archives and Local Studies Library. Walker's Tannery, which was demolished in the 1950s, straddled both sides of the street and was linked by a covered, wooden bridge. The Union Hall was the administration office for the Poor Law Union, a forerunner of income support. The Union was funded by the Poor Law Rate which was paid by the more fortunate citizens of Whitehaven and was the only source of help available to the town's needy and out of work. Today The Union Hall is used as the district office of the Local Education Department of the county council.

Strand Street, at one time little more than a narrow lane, is an important part of the inner ring road without which there would be total traffic chaos. These images give some idea of the scale of redevelopment needed to bring relief to the motorist and pedestrian alike. All the property on the right was demolished and the road widened in the early 1960s. The whole of Mark Lane was razed to the ground and replaced by a single building used by the DSS and the Inland Revenue. The latter has recently moved to Blencathra House on the dock side and Mark House has been earmarked for a much needed hotel. This wholesale razing of property included the Seamen's Bethel, home of Whitehaven Kodak and Rambling Club for many years and Whitehaven Mountain Search and Rescue Team in the 1950s. The Wheatsheaf Hotel and the Ship Inn also fell to the bulldozer with the former becoming part of the ring road and the latter reappearing as the Paul Jones tavern. In their earlier days both pubs shared the same outside gents toilets. After a few pints many a wrong door would be opened – much to the amusement of all concerned. Having widened the street, the county council have just completed the job of narrowing it again!

One glance is sufficient to show the changes which have occurred to the northern end of Tangier Street between 1890 and 1999. The imposing Bransty Arch was used in 1804 to convey coal from James Pit to the harbour side for onward shipment to Dublin. Considered a traffic hazard as early as 1927, the local council ordered its demolition despite intense local opposition and a petition with over 3,000 signatures. The arch was pulled down during March of that year! The shops on the left of the older picture are just a memory now, they included A. & H. Rea (manufacturing confectioners), Mr Martin Hexham, R.D. Leech (fishmonger) and William Workman (china and glass dealers). Today they are replaced by Crosby's fish and chip shop and The Ali Taj Indian restaurant.

Taken at the time of the demolition of the Bransty Arch (March 1927), the older photograph looks south down Tangier Street. Tucked in behind the arch, on the left, is the Crown and Anchor Inn which closed in the 1950s when Brackenthwaite and Hartley Streets (the latter was absorbed into George Street) were cleared for road widening. The taller building in the background housed the Cleator Moor Co-op's butchery, furnishing, drapery and footwear departments. The Co-op also had a popular café upstairs, which is now a photographer's studio. Occupying the ground floor are a fishing tackle shop and a pizza parlour. Note the drinking fountain on the right side of the arch. A similar one is now located on Lowther Street near to the Flat Walks.

The Globe Hotel, one of the town's old coaching inns, was still a popular watering hole in 1964 and did not close its doors until just a few years ago. Tangier Street used to be the main road south through the town with traffic flowing in both directions, note the signposting to Barrow and St Bees. Bill Stainton's sweet shop would remain open until the second house at the Gaiety Cinema had started. Next door, Kerr's Tangier Street post office still functions today as a post office and newsagent and is run by the Hailes family while Stainton's sweet shop has been replaced by the Pat-A-Cake bakery. The older image shows no fewer than three cigarette machines outside Stainton's – what price them lasting five minutes today?

Chapter 3

The Mining Industry

Sunk between 1729 and 1731 to a depth of 439 feet and 6 inches, Saltom Pit was the first mine in the world to have its workings entirely under the sea. On completion of the shaft the team of six sinkers were given a bonus of £6 between them and ale was provided at 'the coaling of the pit'. The total cost incurred by the time that the first coal was produced was £1,907 14s 7¾d. Although this was a high figure, it was worthwhile given that Saltom Pit produced 270,000 tons of coal between 1734 and 1751. There were two salt pans attached to the mine workings capable of producing thirty-six bushels of dry sea salt per day and in the early days the pit made considerably more profit from salt than from coal!

Saltom was originally sunk to drain Lowthers other pits on the landward side. Early visitors to Saltom marvelled at its undersea workings, which by 1756 had extended to three-quarters of a mile. The pit continued at full production until 1848; today it is the most important of Cumbria's industrial monuments. The disused pit buildings, the fireman's cottage and mine offices were still in good condition in the 1930s and the beach was popular with bathers and fishermen alike. Today very little remains apart from the shell of the original engine house and a methane vent at the top of the capped shaft – even this is under threat from subsidence and an unstable cliff.

Wellington Pit was sunk in 1847 and despite a large number of explosions and fires (the worst, in 1910, killed 134 men and boys), the pit produced coal until its closure in 1932. At its peak of production, around 1900, the pit was surrounded with large spoil heaps spewing directly onto the shore. The banks, as they were known, were often covered with people gathering scraps of coal. Poverty in Whitehaven made this task imperative to ensure the family had a fire for warmth and cooking. In the 1950s the banks were removed and by 1975 the area had been landscaped for recreational use. Only the Wellington Lodge remains and after a period as a popular café is now the headquarters of the local coastguard.

William Pit has been described by Ray Devlin and Harry Fancy, in their book on the history of the mine, as 'The Most Dangerous Pit in the Kingdom'. This is no exaggeration – over 300 men, women and children died in the pit before it was closed in 1955. William Pit was sunk in 1804 and raised coal for more than 150 years with the workings reaching out almost 5 miles beneath the Irish Sea. All that remains to show the existence of a once great coal mine is a monument, which was set in place to mark the 50th anniversary of the last great explosion in William Pit in which 104 mine workers perished on the 15 August 1947. The memorial commemorates all those who died beneath the sea throughout the life of the pit.

Sunk in 1914, Haig Pit was the last deep mine to produce coal from the Whitehaven Colliery and, by local standards, it had a short life span (1914 to 1986). Haig too had its share of disasters in which more than 100 men and boys died; 14 of whom remain entombed in the pit beneath the Irish Sea. All that remains of Haig today is the winding engine and power houses, the rest of the surface buildings have been demolished to accommodate a number of small workshops which were intended to attract small manufacturing companies to the area who would then provide employment for the redundant miners. Unfortunately, 10 years on barely half of these units have been occupied and very few of the 650 former miners have found work there.

The introduction of mechanised coal handling, washing and separation facilities in 1982 was a last ditch attempt to save Haig Pit from closing. Part of the scheme involved bringing the coal to the surface in an endless stream of skips. The final tubs of coal were brought to the surface in July 1982. This expensive development was not enough to save the pit and it closed in January 1986, bringing to an end all deep coal mining in Cumbria. Today the steam winding engines, which were left under a heavy coat of grease, are being restored to their former glory by The Haig Pit Restoration Group, who intend to open a mining museum in the old engine houses. Some funding towards a new roof has been secured by the group and work on this is underway.

Coal was not the only mineral to be mined in Whitehaven, alabaster and anhydrite were also extracted from the ground in considerable quantities. Alabaster is a semi-transparent, soft, white stone used in the manufacture of plaster and cement, and for decorative carving. The stone was worked at Barrowmouth where entrance to the mine was gained by a bearmouth – in 1921 it also provided easy access for the exploring student of geology. Anhydrite was produced by Marchon Products Ltd at their Solway Mine, where access to the workings was by way of a long drift. In the twenty-five years or so of its life approximately 10 million tons of anhydrite were produced, for conversion into sulphuric acid and cement.

Unlike coal, anhydrite is a hard rock and can be mined without the danger of an explosion of firedamp (methane). These factors allow the use of heavy motorised drilling, handling and transport equipment in the mine. In May 1962 we see drilling prior to the insertion of explosives to fracture the rock and allow its removal from the face. With the closure of the mine in the late 1970s, the only form of mining left in West Cumbria was the opencast extraction of coal. Opencast mining, as its name implies, involves opening up a massive hole in the ground to reach the coal measures, which are then extracted by large excavators. The picture shows the scale of operations at one such mine at Tattie Pot Lane.

Chapter 4

Education and Social Welfare

The foundation stone for St Beghs Roman Catholic church on Coach Road was laid in 1865 and the church opened for worship on 9 October 1868. The west door of this beautiful church is lined with alabaster and the building once had a belfry surmounted with a large metal cross. Safety considerations made it necessary to remove this feature leaving the church with just a single bell. The first ordination in Whitehaven in over 200 years took place at St Beghs on Sunday 25 July 1931, when Revd Father V. Fallona was ordained by the Bishop of Lancaster.

The Marine School was founded in 1817 by local benefactor, Mathew Piper, for the education of sixty poor boys, resident in Whitehaven, in reading, writing, arithmetic, gauging, navigation and bookkeeping. The school was in High Street and accepted boys aged eight and over, for a maximum period of five years, provided that they could read the New Testament. The school thus prepared boys for the position of mate or master should they wish to follow a life at sea. The building was sold in 1908 and the money raised was used to purchase the site of the County Secondary School in Catherine Street. Compare the relative class and year group sizes with that of a recent year 11 at Whitehaven School.

The two buildings of the Irish Street School were erected by the local council in 1911, at a cost of £20,000, and replaced the old St Nicholas School on Scotch Street. The older view is of the smaller of the two school buildings (the infant school) seen here soon after the school opened. The group of youngsters and parents differs little from the scene outside any of today's infant schools, with one youngster clinging to mother's skirt while the rest show total indifference. It almost goes without saying that all would have walked to school on that day. The school building is now used by the Social Services Department of the county council, the bricks and mortar of the building have not changed over the past eighty-five years.

Whitehaven County Secondary School was built in 1908, taking pupils who passed the eleven plus examination along with some fee-paying students. The school was upgraded to a grammar school in the mid-1940s and discipline was strict with the wearing of school uniform mandatory. In 1966 a new grammar school was erected at Hensingham, in keeping with the new comprehensive education theories of the time. The old school building was soon occupied by the staff and pupils of Irish Street School (by then renamed Richmond Secondary Modern School). During the early 1980s all the pupils from The Kells, Lillyhall, Ehenside, Richmond and Hensingham Secondary Modern Schools were merged with the new grammar school to form Whitehaven School. The old grammar school buildings have now been demolished and the site is occupied by the new Safeway superstore.

The Mission of St Gregory and St Patrick was erected in 1890 and had an infant school added in 1889, this continued to provide an early education for many of the town's children until 1960. To the right are many of the streets and buildings which formed part of the old town including Quay Street, Bardy Lane, James Place and Littledale Lane. These old streets contained some well known public houses including The Manx Arms, Braddylls Arms, The Crown and Mitre and The Union Jack. Almost all of the buildings on Quay Street have given way to redevelopment. The Duke Pit has been subject to a degree of conservation, while the Mission of St Gregory and St Patrick continues to serve many of the towns older residents.

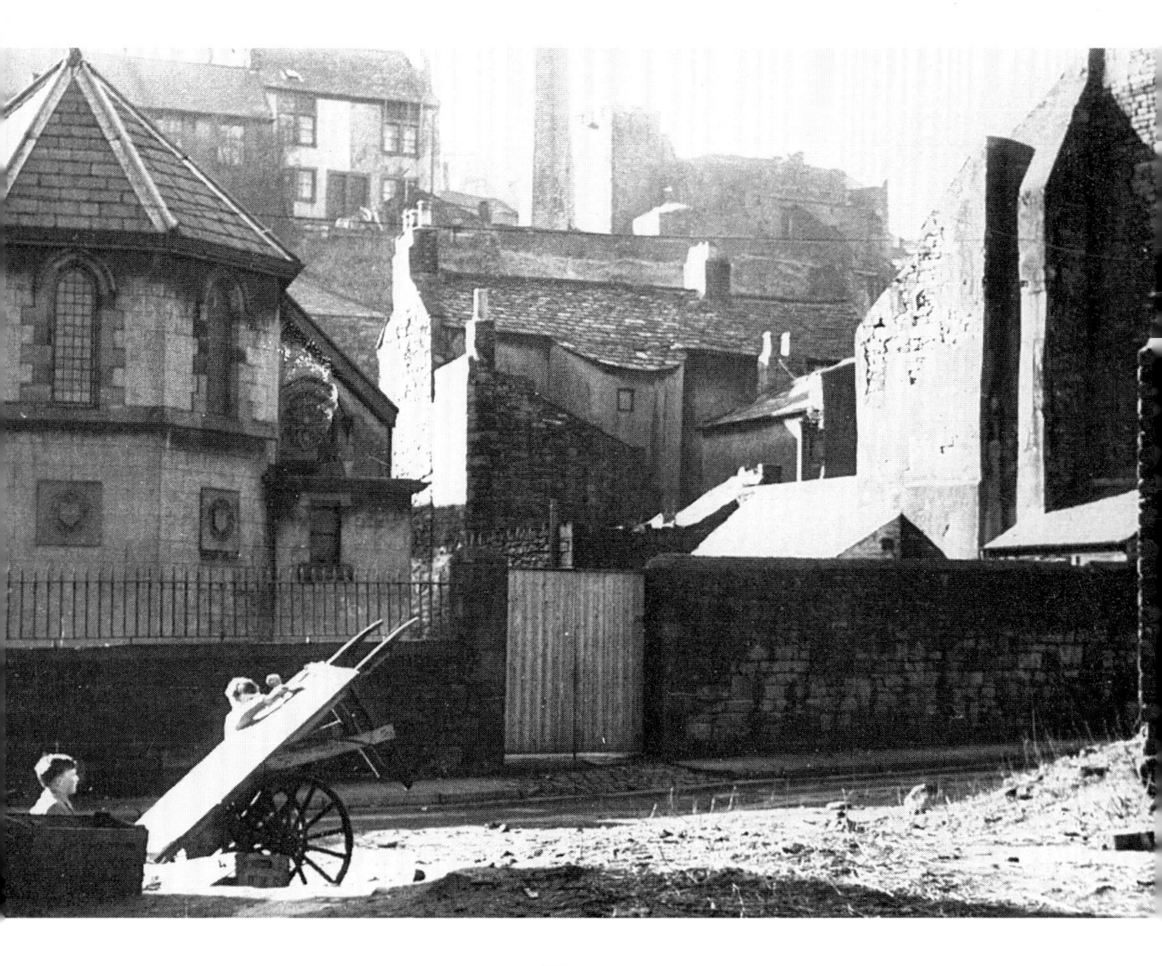

Following the demolition of Holy Trinity in 1949 a beautiful wrought iron screen (which surrounded Sir James Lowther's memorial) was erected as the Duke Street entrance to St Nicholas church and a quiet garden was created where the Trinity church once stood. Trinity Gardens are the wedding photographer's dream, placed as they are within just a few yards of the local registry office, they allow the taking of those photographs that are so essential to the bride and groom's 'big day'. Without the dominating presence of the church the view up Roper Street past Daniel Brocklebank's house (left) is open to the castle and the technical college (unfortunately this is to be demolished in order to make way for yet another drive-in fast food outlet.)

Built between July 1713 and March 1714, Holy Trinity church stood at the head of Roper Street. The building, originally named King Georges church, broke through the walls surrounding the grounds of the Flatt and was set well away from the town centre. The church numbered many of Whitehaven's more prosperous citizens among its congregation and the older photograph gives some indication of the worth of some townsfolk – their offspring were looked after by uniformed nannies.

The land surrounding St Nicholas church was used mainly as a burial ground, however when the new cemetery, on the St Bees Road, opened and pressure on the churchyard lessened the grounds were turned into a quiet garden which opened to the public on Tuesday 15 June 1920. To mark the occasion Mrs Herbert W. Walker, wife of the town's leading benefactor planted a tree. Accompanying her is the mayor, Alderman B. Palmer CC and looking on (right) is her husband. In the background are the backs of houses and shops on Duke Street which were pulled down in the road widening schemes of the 1950s. Today the gardens have been greatly improved and are a haven of peace and beauty in the busy town centre. The widow Mildred Washington, who married local merchant John Gale in 1699, lies buried in the church grounds. She had three children by her first husband; Joan, Augustine and Mildred. Augustine remained in America where he married and became the father of George Washington – the first of a long line of presidents of the United States of America.

Prior to 1693 the only place of worship in Whitehaven was a little chapel which lay across the junction of Lowther Street and Chapel Street. At that time a new church (St Nicholas) was erected in Lowther Street and it served the community well for almost 200 years. The old church was demolished in 1881 and replaced by a bigger building which, in turn, was destroyed by a spectacular fire on the afternoon of 31 August 1971. A building fund was immediately established but the fine old church was never rebuilt although the clock tower has been converted into a café and visitor centre. The grounds are kept up to a high standard, helping Whitehaven to complete successfully in the Britain in Bloom competition.

James Hogarth, a local weaving mill owner, built The Mission at the junction of The Mount and Rosemary Lane for his workforce. The Mission was later used by the Michael Street Methodists and also provided a temporary home for Whitehaven's Primative Methodists at which time it was nicknamed the Ranters Chapel. After a short period of use as a candle factory, the building was purchased by the Wesleyan Methodists and remained as a place of worship until 1954 when slum clearance and falling congregations made its closure inevitable. Crossthwaite School canteen was erected in its place. Now the site is part of the Mount Recreation Area and affords a particularly good view over the town and harbour.

Sir James Lowther planned to build 500 houses near the Ginns, for his miners. A total of 266 were completed by 1788 and were known as the New Houses. Built into the side of a hill the three rows had no toilets or running water and the lady of the house often had to fetch water from more than a mile away. They were served by twenty-one ash pits where night-soil was dumped. Following a long period of fever and disease, the 1860s saw running water piped to the town and a rudimentary form of sewerage disposal introduced. The older image (from around 1900) shows the front row with their outside privies – one shared between four houses. By 1940 all the residents had been rehoused in new council properties on the outskirts of town. Today this same row of houses is being partially restored as part of a local history and tourism project.

The welfare of the miner and the factory worker has improved over the years. In the mining industry it took some time for pithead baths and the like to become the norm. It was not until 1941 that the Haig Pit miners had the benefit of baths and changing rooms, a medical centre and a canteen. The older photograph was taken at the opening of the new canteen. Marchon, on the other hand, had what was reputed to be the best works canteen in Northern Britain. Drivers and visitors for miles around used to make a bee-line for Marchon at lunch time. Today the canteen has been moved and self-service has been introduced.

The Whitehaven Unemployed and Working Mens Club was located at the corner of Strand and Marlborough Streets. Earlier occupants of the premises included, in 1780, Charles Dickinson (hatter); 1864, William Williamson (tailor and outfitter); 1884, Hewitson Hurst (clogger and pattern maker); and in 1901, E.J. Bridsons Manx Bakery. The WU&WC made use of the premises up to their demolition in the late 1950s and a large part of the corner is now occupied by a fun pub The Whitehouse. This replaced an earlier building, erected on stilts and used as a meeting place for The Royal and Ancient Order of Buffalos. It has had a string of names as it moved into night time entertainment including The Zodiak Club, The Talk of the North and The Whitehouse. Most of Marlborough Street was pulled down at the time the RAOB were building their new club. The short street contained several pubs and small warehouses which became workshops like Dick Eliott's radio and television repair shop. Today the street has a new restaurant – The American Connection, and a wine merchant – Richardson's. Both businesses are nicely located near the harbour side to take advantage of further quayside developments.

Chapter 5

Shipbuilding and Safety at Sea

A large sailing vessel under construction in the old Brocklebanks Yard, *c.* 1875. The Wellington Pit and The Howgill Wagonway can be clearly seen towards the right of the picture and there is some activity around the Queens Dock. This appears to be work on the later stages of construction of the dock gates and thus helps us to date the photograph.

Daniel Brocklebank established a shipbuilding yard in Whitehaven in 1782, almost seven years after he quit his yard at Sheepscutt, Maine. Brocklebank, a merchant trader who built ships for his own use, was succeeded by his sons, Thomas and John who gave their names to one of the most famous shipping lines of all time T. & J. Brocklebank. They transferred their interests to Liverpool in 1855 and sold their yard to William Huddart. The yard soon passed into the hands of the Whitehaven Shipbuilding Company No. 1 and later No. 2, who built the two biggest ships ever to be launched in Whitehaven the *Alice A. Liegh* and the *Englehorn*. The old photograph shows the *Alice* on the stocks on the day of her launch in October 1889. Today the site is occupied by the disused Dawnfresh Fish Processing Factory, though a new fish market is planned for the site.

The launch of the *Alice A. Liegh* took place in October 1889 and was a big disappointment to everyone concerned. The big barque – at 2,929 tons the biggest vessel ever built at Whitehaven – stayed put in the stocks. Constructed for J. Joyce and Company of Liverpool, the *Alice* cost £25,943 to build and a great deal extra to get into the water. A similar experience with her sister ship, the *Englehorn*, confirmed the futility of building bigger and bigger vessels in Whitehaven and brought to an end well over 200 years of shipbuilding in the town. No fewer than three steam-powered paddle tugs stained to drag the *Alice* into the water. Today the only launching to be seen in the town is at the new 45 ton boat lift at the Queens Dock.

Wood from Scandinavia (especially Norway) was imported from the seventeenth century until the 1980s and many of the town's merchants used their vessels in trade with the Baltic states. They imported pitch, tar, timber, hemp, whale oil, linseed and flax; materials which found a ready market in the industries of the town. The older image, from the 1890s, shows two timber ships, the *Basspeaks* and another, tied up in the Queens Dock. Many fine buildings have been lost to the developer from around the dock side, the most important of which were the dock offices and clock tower. In their stead came the Marchon Silos and conveyor system, which also offered little resistance to the demolition experts when their useful life came to an end.

Tied up at the end of the Sugar Tongue and getting ready to sail, the small vessel is typical of many which used Whitehaven towards the end of the nineteenth century. The barrels on the deck could have contained anything from brandy to rabbit skins but in this case they probably contained salt for laying down herrings. Behind the vessel is The Wellington Pit and a handful of houses built around the Wellington Inn and the Steam Tug Tavern. In the 1950s the pit spoil heaps were removed and used to build the standing areas at the recreation ground, home of Whitehaven Warriors Rugby League Football Club, and The Lodge was converted into a café by the local council in the early 1970s.During the weekend of 26 and 27 June 1999, this south side of the harbour was the setting for the Whitehaven Maritime Festival, attended by no less than 80,000 spectators. A wide variety of tall ships, ocean going yachts, vintage vessels and a 9 metre model of an aircraft carrier took part. A re-enactment of John Paul Jones' raid on the harbour during the American war of independence was carried out against a backdrop of fireworks and a monumental thunderstorm. At the same time the USA received an official pardon for the raid. The event will be repeated in the year 2001.

The *Dunboyne*, a vessel of 1,355 tons, was built by the Whitehaven Shipbuilding Company in the old T. & J. Brocklebank Yards and launched on 28 February 1888. The vessel is tied up in the Queens Dock and attended by a number of steam powered cranes; these small but proficient lifting devices remained in constant use around the Queens Dock until well after the Second World War. The vessel changed hands a couple of times and was at one time known as the *G.O. Kennedy*, before finally becoming the *Af. Chapman*. By 1937 she was based in Sweden, where she remains to this day. The smaller photograph shows her laying off Stockholm harbour, restored to her former glory and operating as a youth training vessel.

A look around Whitehaven's graveyards will quickly show just how dangerous the Irish Sea can be 'Lost at sea in a gale of wind' is a typical inscription on a family headstone. The harbour has never been easy to enter and high spring tides pushed by equinoctial gales make the task impossible. Of course for the modern tourist the sight of great waves breaking in a spectacular manner over the piers is inspiring. The fate of a skipper and his crew, caught in such a sea, is well depicted in the picture from the 1880s when a large vessel was blown onto the rocks at Parton, just north of the harbour. When a ship was wrecked it was the skill and bravery of the Rocket Brigade which led to a successful rescue.

The Rocket Brigade were originally stationed on the Old Quay and later on the Old New Quay. Formed in 1849 the brigade was equipped with six Patent Rockets and Rocket Lines. An attempt was made in 1891 to move them to St Bees but in the end the brigade remained in Whitehaven and to this day their successors, the coastguard, are still stationed here. For many years Whitehaven Sea Cadets have occupied buildings on the Old New Quay (the TS Bee). In its hey day the Rocket Brigade boasted more than twenty-five men trained to the required standard and available twenty-four hours a day. Today's coastguard station has one full time officer who looks after much of the Cumbrian coastline and he is backed up by a force of volunteers, their operations being co-ordinated by the regional office in Liverpool.

Following a series of losses at sea during 1790, the town and harbour commissioners were obliged to provide a lifeboat in a belated attempt to placate the town's merchants and seafarers. They ordered a boat of the largest size from Henry Greathead of South Shields. The boat was hauled overland to Whitehaven and stationed on the North Shore. Miss Elizabeth Leicester from London presented the crew with a new boat in 1866 and three years later the *Elizabeth* became part of the RNLI. The *Elizabeth* and her successor the *Elizabeth Leicester II* were often launched to go to the assistance of a vessel in distress, a feat which took some effort. Whitehaven lost its own lifeboat in 1925 and has since been serviced by the Workington boat, seen here in Whitehaven harbour in 1998.

Built in 1903, the *Elizabeth Leicester II* saved many lives before the RNLI decided to close the Whitehaven Station for good in 1925. Typical of these acts bravery was the rescue of the crew of the *Ellen and Mary* in October 1921. All the crew were rowed to safety but unfortunately the vessel sank off Whitehaven. These days inshore rescue is the province of the high speed inflatable boats such as those stationed at Silloth, Maryport and St Bees. Most of their call-outs come from small pleasure craft or the occasional fishing boat usually with a failed engine, damaged rudder or the like. The Maryport boat heads out into the Solway Firth after action off Whitehaven where casualties are often landed to be taken to the West Cumberland Hospital.

Chapter 6

Entertainment and Leisure

Whitehaven has seen few greater causes for a knees up than the end of the Second World War. In common with every other town and village in Britain, the people of Whitehaven had suffered through a lean time, with shortages and rationing common place. Despite the fact that coal mining was a reserved occupation many men volunteered for active service with the county regiment who were heavily involved in Burma (the Chindits) and in Europe, especially at Arnhem and Sicily. Husbands and sons were killed or became POWs and the end of the conflict was a great relief to all. The inhabitants of Cross Street and its surrounds celebrated with a whale of a street party!

Located at the harbour end of Marlborough Street, The Little Sands and Duncan Square were popular places for children to play or have a paddle after school or on a Sunday afternoon, *c.* 1930. Marlborough Street was one of the shortest streets in town and had barely twenty properties along its length. It had a disproportionate number of pubs per resident – the Solway Vaults was one of the more popular among them. Virtually all of the properties on Marlborough Street have been demolished and replaced with small workshops. Duncan Square (on the right) has been restored with properties converted into flats. Today the harbour is under water at all times, The Little Sands remains a permanent feature though the swimming is left to the swans.

Judging from the crowds in the 1870s Whitehaven's Annual Regatta was a spectacular affair! All the vantage points were taken up long before the event began. There were races for fishing and pilot boats, races for half-decked sailing boats, races for rowing boats and races for swimming. There was a shovel race for trimmers and dockers and a ham was offered to anyone who could walk the greasy bowsprit. A Whitehaven Regatta still takes place but in a limited way with sailing races held round a triangular course outside the harbour confines each year. With the revitalisation of the harbour and the emphasis on leisure activity, an attempt to stage a water-based weekend of festivity is planned for 1999. This year should also see the harbour becoming a regular stop-over for boat and crews taking part in the annual round Britain yacht race.

The Empire Cinema was a single-storey building with entrances in both Roper and Chapel Streets, the latter to what was known locally as 'The Dog End'. The layout of the Empire was totally unsuitable for a cinema with only the most expensive seats getting a decent view and it was the first of the town's cinemas to feel the pinch of falling audiences. It turned to bingo instead and became The Tombola Club. A visit to The McConnell Brothers Outdoor Clothing and Footwear Shop, was an education, such was the apparent state of chaos! The brothers, however, knew exactly where to find what was needed to leave the customer totally satisfied. Recently demolished, the site is now occupied by a variety of businesses including a hairdresser, a café and The Whitehaven Warriors fund-raising shop.

The stage has been a source of entertainment and enjoyment in Whitehaven from as early as 1734, when John Hayton opened the Assembly Rooms in Howgill Street. Later came the Theatre Royal and The Music Hall at the Shakespeare Hotel, both in Roper Street. The Royal Standard Hotel on the West Strand had a music hall added by the then owner, Hamilton Dixon, in the 1800s. Sadly all of these places of entertainment have gone. The Queens Cinema provided a platform for many of Whitehaven's amateur productions in the 1930s, '40s and '50s, a need met today by both the Rosehill Theatre and the Civic Hall. *Katrina* was a typical production of the '30s; *The Wizard of Oz* was the one of the latest productions of the Whitehaven Operatic Society.

Music has long been a source of relaxation, inspiration and pleasure; marching bands in particular tend to inspire the soldier and spectator. Whitehaven is no exception having, over the years, been home to several military, church and town bands. In former days the Borough Band was a large one and performed at many functions including the local carnival and marching at the front of the Lifeboat Parade. Formed up in the park, the band prepares to march off around 1900. One function always supported by a band was the Mayors Sunday Parade, on recent occasions this has been the preserve of either the Borough Band or the band of the Kings Own Royal Border Regiment TA.

Dance music plays an important part in everyday life and at one time there were several good dance bands in the town, sadly, this is no longer the case. One of the earliest dance bands was Jackson's Exelda Dance Band with Mr Jackson himself on piano, Roy Lilly on drums and percussion, and Mrs McMillan on violin. In addition to playing for local dances the orchestra also played, on occasion, at the Theatre Royal. When the Empress Ballroom was opened in the 1930s the Exelda Dance Band became the founder members of the renowned Empress Rhythm Aces, which outplayed some of the country's biggest named dance bands when they occasionally performed at the Empress Ballroom.

The Grand Hotel was one of the major hotels in northern Britain. The hotel was built in 1846/47 by the then Lord Lonsdale and named after him, however, within a few years the hotel was used as the offices of the Whitehaven and Furness Junction Railway. Once Bransty Station was rebuilt, The Grand re-opened as a hotel and continued as such until it was burned out on the morning of the 21 January 1940. The Grand possessed a magnificent ballroom which was the scene of many a brilliant gathering and, following the Incorporation of Whitehaven into a Borough on 11 July 1894, was the venue for a reception for the new Mayor and Mayoress, The Lord and Lady Lonsdale. Today there is nothing to show that The Grand Hotel once stood in what is now Tescos car park.

Playing or watching Rugby League Football at both the amateur and professional level has been part of Whitehaven's sporting scene for more than fifty years. Apart from the Ford Northern Premiership professional club, Whitehaven Warriors, the town has two top class amateur sides Hensingham and Kells. Both clubs have made it to the first round proper of the Rugby League Challenge Cup on several occasions. Both photographs are of Kells, the newest is of one of several youth teams run by the club and the older depicts the team which played Warrington in the cup in 1946. From left to right, back row: E. Proud, H. Crellin (reserves), G. Bethwaite (committee), N. Baily (reserve), W.J. Walker (committee), T. Chilton (reserve), W. Walker (treasurer), J. Heslop (committee). Second row: J. Shanks (committee), D. Underwood (trainer), W. Eaves (committee), J.H. Graham, R. McFarlane, H. Chilton, W. Lowe and R. Young (committee), W.W. Moore (secretary), W. Proud (committee). Seated: J. Buchannan, W.E. Rodgers, W. Mullholand, J. Norman, T. Stewart (captain and chairman), L. Buchannan, J. Gabriel, V. Young. In front: A. Buchannan and T. Proud.

The Red Flag Inn, *c.* 1904. This was one of Whitehaven's oldest inns and was originally called the High Bowling Green Inn. The picture dates from just before the pub was forced to close after the local police objected to the renewal of its license. The pub was alleged to be unsupervisable, that is there were too many routes for after hours drinkers and gamblers to escape arrest and prosecution. The Bowling Green Inn had one other tenuous claim to fame in that it is said that Jonathan Swift (author of Gulliver's Travels) was taken there by his nanny when a child. This is commemorated today by calling the building Jonathan Swift House. Unfortunately the house has become dilapidated over the years and is in need of major restoration.

Sailors and miners are renowned the world over for their capacity to consume large quantities of ale and the men of Whitehaven were no different – drinking home-brewed beers at first and later the beverages available down at their local pub. Many of Whitehaven's pubs were situated close to areas of high population density and the Blacksmiths Arms was typical of this trend, lying at the foot of The Mount alongside The Blue Anchor and The Lighthouse Inn. The Blacksmiths Arms had its license rescinded and was referred to the compensation board in 1921, ten years or so after this photograph was taken. The Blue Anchor was the first to be closed in 1906 while The Lighthouse survived until 1931. The West Strand site of all three pubs has been recently developed into the Beacon complex.

The Castle View Inn was known as The Stump to its regulars for most of its life, either because it was supposedly built on the stump of an old windmill or because an early landlord had a wooden stump for a leg. Whatever the reason it is now licensed as The Stump. Standing high on Prospect it has a fine view of the castle. It was a man's pub, with manual workers in the bar and white-collar workers in 'The Room'; these groups rarely mixed, except when the Bow Tie Club met. Some of the members of the club pose for a photograph prior to a trip to the races, around 1966. Today there is no separation of customers who crowd the bar to watch a football match on TV.

Chapter 7

Local Industries

Along with mining and shipbuilding, Whitehaven has seen many other types of industry come and go. Salt panning, iron smelting, glass and pottery making, tanning, sugar refining and manufacture of tobacco based products have all been replaced by chemical, nuclear and other high tech operations. The North Shore is now a quiet promenade but in 1900 it was a hive of activity. From left to right are: The Lonsdale Iron works, Henry and William Pits, the coke ovens and the gasworks. Slag and waste from these works was dumped directly onto the shore in the hope that sea and wave power would disperse them. Today this would not be acceptable, though at the time it did not seem to deter the Sunday bathers.

The Lonsdale Haematite Iron Company Works, *c.* 1890. The works were located north of William Pit and at the foot of Bransty cliffs. The three blast furnaces were capable of smelting a total of 2,100 tons of iron per week. The company ceased production in 1902 and was liquidated in 1904. All that can be seen of these ironworks today is the slag bank, or Whitey Rock as it known locally. The rock was to have been the location of a major piece of sculpture by the world renowned artist Eduardo Chillada (who works in steel) and it would have been a fitting place for a great work, however, local opinion favoured a memorial to coal mining and the sculpture was lost.

W. & T. Ramsey, iron founders were established in the 1860s and operated the Pheonix Foundry in Albion Street. This engraving from around 1895 gives some idea of the size of the works at that time. The premises were later occupied by Peter Hanratty, a marine stores and general dealer who in time added the occupation of scrap metal dealer to his long list of business activities. Succeeded by his son Bernard and in turn by grandson Peter, the scrap business still thrives today. The four-storey warehouse to the right of the property can still be recognised though, with the exception of the foundry chimney, the rest of the buildings have either gone or been altered.

Another long established engineering company was that of J. Stout and Sons Ltd (formerly Pearts Engineering) who operated the Newtown Foundry for many years, working in iron and brass. The foundry continued to manufacture high grade castings until the 1980s, before the premises were taken over for use first as a carpet warehouse and later a car showroom and garage services. The property was demolished in 1997 and the site partially cleared for commercial redevelopment. The earlier photograph was taken in 1968 when the foundry was nearing the end of its useful life. During demolition evidence of earlier industrial use of the site was found.

In addition to the metal worked and in order to operate to full capacity, the successful engineering business needed a whole range of other equipment and materials. One supplier of such was Andrew A. McArd & Co. of Williamsons Lane. The inside of his warehouse is seen here around 1895. McArds described their business as 'Engineers Furnishers, Oil and Colourmen, Iron, Steel and Metal Merchants'. Certainly their premises are stacked with ropes, chains, blocks and tackle, grindstones, pipes and joints, lamps, cans and measures; indeed anything and everything that could possibly be required. The nearest equivalent business in town today is that of R. Robinson in Tangier Street who also have a substantial range of tools and hardware on offer.

The manufacture of pottery was one of the first industries to be developed in the town. On a small scale at first and probably in the market area of the town, pottery manufacture took on a greater significance when Whitehaven started to trade with the West Indies and the American colonies. This trade sometimes involved a trip to Africa for slaves and pottery was a standard trading requirement. This need for more pots led to the establishment of a number of factories in and around the Ginns. The older image, from around 1900, is of the John Wilkinsons works in Pottery Road. In later years the old buildings were converted into a slaughterhouse which operated for many years. Today the old pottery buildings house a variety of small businesses.

The tannery on Scotch Street, *c.* 1920. This was founded by George Miller in 1764 and eventually sold to William Walker in 1858, being successfully worked by the Walker family until its closure in 1958. Perhaps the most important member of the family was Herbert Wilson Walker, who was a great benefactor to the town. He purchased the castle and then donated it to the people of Whitehaven for use as a hospital. Soon after its closure the tannery was demolished along with most of the surrounding area as part of a slum clearance programme. New flats were built in an attempt to keep a residential area in the town centre. A car showroom and garage occupy part of the tannery site.

An essential support industry in the early days of coal mining and the fishing industry was that of basket making. Crans for fish, baskets for lowering men and equipment down the mine and to bring coal from the face to the eye of the pit and on up the shaft were all needed in quantity. One basket maker was located at Kells (Arrowthwaite), within walking distance of several pits including Croft, Kells, King, Duke, Ravenhill, Thwaite and Saltom. Later Mary Telford and her mother ran Basket House (seen here around 1965) as a corner shop. It was deemed a traffic hazard by the council at that time and was pulled down for road widening. Today, almost twenty years later, the site remains untouched – another historic building lost for no good reason.

In December 1939 Frank Schon and Fred Marzillier formed a small trading company in London called Marchon Products Limited. After being caught up in the German bombing of London they moved to Whitehaven and began to make firelighters in 1941. After a spell in the Guinea Warehouse they moved into the largely disused Ladysmith Pit at Kells in 1943. Some of the former pit buildings continued to be used for coal washing and wagon repairs by the NCB. Seen here in 1970, these old buildings were later demolished to allow for the construction of a large phosphate rock storage and handling facility. Today the site is used as a lagoon for the treatment of waste water from the chemical works before it is discharged into the sea.

Lab. 3 at Marchon, *c.* 1954. This was one of a number of redundant buildings purchased from the Ministry of Defence TNT works at Sellafield in the late 1940s. For many years it was the home of the research and development, routine analysis and technical service departments. The two-storey white building in the background was the newly built (in 1951) Kells Secondary Modern School which closed after a mere twenty-five years and has now been pulled down to make way for a housing development. In those early years the Marchon factory expanded at a phenomenal rate and today's photograph gives some indication of that growth. Lab. 3 has long since been demolished and many of its original functions are now carried out at the parent company works in Birmingham.

Marchon Products Limited was a world pioneer in the field of detergents and in the 1950s one thing the housewife looked for in her washing powder was a good head of foam. The foaming agent (active ingredient) was made on site by sulphonating dodcylbenzene with super strong sulphuric acid, springing the sulphonic acid from the spent acid and neutralising with caustic soda. The quantities (flow rates) of the reactants were controlled by flowmeters being adjusted by the worker on the right. The acidity or alkalinity was monitored and adjusted by the chargehand worker (left). Today the computer has taken over and process control has been much simplified.

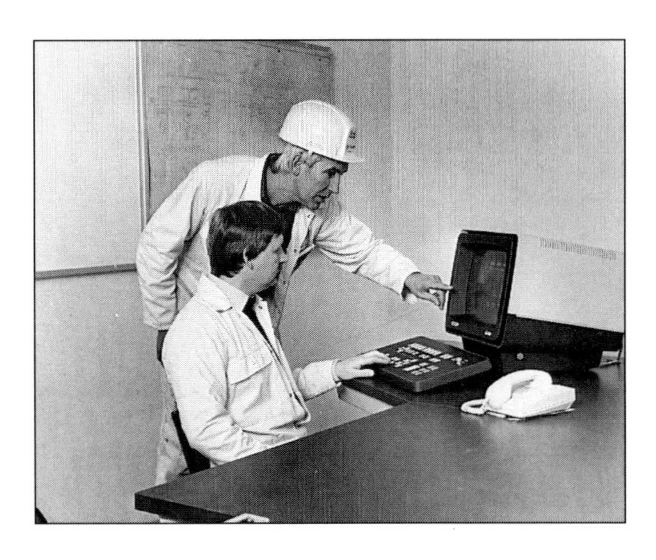

In the early days at Marchon many of the chemical raw materials were delivered in 45 gallons drums and had to be manhandled into the processing areas. This was a time of growing trade unionism and strict job demarcation; lifting was riggers work. The setting up of a block and tackle required the expert hand of the rigger and in the 1960s David Cradduck (above right) was often called to help his workmates in the processing units. The finished product was also packed and sold in drums as it still is today in some cases. Modern drum handling facilities demonstrate the semi-automatic nature of the work today.

From the outset Whitehaven was unable to provide enough grain for its population and their animals. So important, therefore, was the shipping of cereals into Whitehaven that vessels bringing grain were given absolute preference to all others when it came to loading coals. In 1855 John Pattinson began milling flour at the old barracks in Catherine Street before moving, in 1906, to Beacon Mills on the former site of Brocklebanks shipyards. For many years grain was brought from Liverpool in Pattinson's own boats; *The Margaret*, *The Clint* and, seen here in the 1940s, *The Busk*. The business was bought by Quaker Oats Limited in 1949 and continued to trade until 1975. The site is expected to undergo redevelopment in the near future into a wholesale fish market.

The inclusion in this volume of a factory some twelve miles south of Whitehaven may be something of a surprise, it is however fully justified. British Nuclear Fuels plc have contributed greatly to change in the area through the provision of employment; up to 13,000 jobs at the peak of construction work and now more than 6,000 permanent jobs. These wage packets alone have had a tremendous effect on local economic well being. The company has also poured a great deal of money into town centre redevelopment and is an active participant in the Whitehaven Development Company. The two images, taken some twenty-five years apart, show clearly the changes which have occurred on the Sellafield site. The original piles, Calder Hall Power Station and the 'golf ball' of the AGR appear on both images. Thorpe, Pond Five, High Active Storage, The Vitrification Plant, The Magnox Unit and a gas-fired power station, among other developments, have been added in the intervening years. At the same time the river Calder has been straightened.